BRITAIN in the INDUSTRIAL REVOLUTION

Fiona Macdonald

W
FRANKLIN WATTS
LONDON•SYDNEY

© 2003 Franklin Watts

First published in 2003 by
Franklin Watts
96 Leonard Street
London
EC2A 4XD

Franklin Watts Australia
45-51 Huntley Street
Alexandria
NSW 2015

ISBN: 0 7496 4869 4

A CIP catalogue record for this book is available from the British Library

Printed in Malaysia
Planning and production by Discovery Books Limited
Editor: Helen Dwyer
Design: Keith Williams
Picture research: Rachel Tisdale

Photographs:
Cover, title page and border Bridgeman Art Library/Trustees of the National Museums
& Galleries on Merseyside, 4 English Heritage/Steve Cole, 5 Mary Evans Picture
Library, 6 Glasgow Museums, 7 Bridgeman Art Library/The Stapleton Collection, 8
Bridgeman Art Library/Guildhall Library, 9 top Mary Evans Picture Library, 9 bottom
Museum of Welsh Life, 10 Glasgow Museums, 11 Museum of Welsh Life, 12
Bridgeman Art Library/Trustees of the National Museums & Galleries on Merseyside,
13 top New Lanark Conservation Trust, 13 bottom, 14 & 15 top Mary Evans Picture
Library, 15 bottom Bridgeman Art Library, 16 Beamish, The North of England Open
Air Museum, 17 Bridgeman Art Library/Guildhall Library, 18 Bridgeman Art
Library/City of Bristol Museum and Art Gallery, 19 & 20 Mary Evans Picture Library,
21 Bridgeman Art Library/The Stapleton Collection, 22 Mary Evans Picture Library,
23 top Bridgeman Art Library/The Stapleton Collection, 23 bottom Mary Evans
Picture Library, 24 Bridgeman Art Library/Victoria & Albert Museum, 25 top Mary
Evans Picture Library, 25 bottom Museum of Welsh Life, 26 New Lanark
Conservation Trust, 27 top Mary Evans Picture Library, 27 bottom Glasgow
Museums, 28 top Ironbridge Gorge Museums Trust, 28 bottom New Lanark
Conservation Trust, 29 English Heritage/Nigel Corrie

BRITAIN in the
INDUSTRIAL REVOLUTION

Contents

Changing Times

This book looks at a period when Britain was changing very fast – between about AD 1750 and 1850. These years are sometimes called the 'Industrial Revolution', because scientists and engineers living at the time invented many new machines that completely transformed people's work and lives.

The new machines were driven by water or steam, and could work much more quickly and efficiently than those powered by humans or animals. The machines were used to pump water, spin thread, weave cloth and make pottery. Machines shaped and hammered metal to make wheels, gates, ships, guns, farm equipment and tools. They were used to **mass-produce** useful items, such as knives and nails, much more cheaply and reliably than before.

Inventors also found new ways to produce useful materials, such as **cast iron** for large buildings and intricate machinery. They experimented with new substances, such as quicker drying, stronger concrete and vulcanized (heat-treated), tougher rubber.

◀ This steam-powered engine was used in the mid-1800s to carve wooden bobbins (spools on which thread was wound) at Stott Park Bobbin Mill in Cumbria. Thousands of new bobbins were needed every year by machines that spun thread and wove cloth in big factories.

British inventors also developed new forms of transport – canals, railways and steamships – to carry **raw materials** to factories, and finished goods to markets and ports. By around 1850, Britain proudly claimed to be 'the workshop of the world'.

▼ This picture from 1831 shows two trains pulled by steam locomotives on the newly opened Liverpool to Manchester railway. They have comfortable, closed carriages for rich passengers, but rough, open-air wagons for poorer travellers.

Factories and towns

The new machines were housed in factories built close to supplies of water, iron ore (rock containing iron) and coal. They needed many workers to operate them. Soon, big cities grew up around the factories, as workers moved there to live. This was the biggest change in lifestyle that British people had ever seen. Before 1750, 8 out of every 10 people lived and worked in the countryside. By 1851, more than half the British population lived and worked in cities and towns.

► This map of Britain shows all the towns that had a population of more than 20,000 in 1801. Fifty years earlier, only London, Bristol and Norwich were that large. Towns grew rapidly as they became centres for new industries, often based on local supplies of coal. Ports grew as they supplied the towns with raw materials and traded their products around the world.

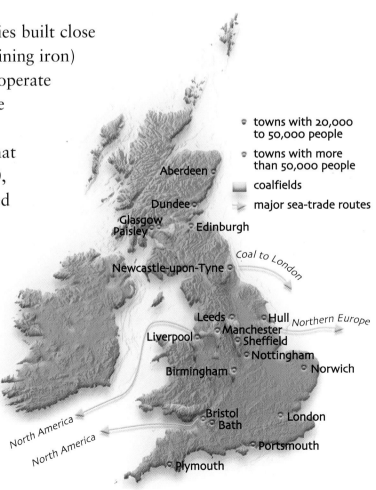

○ towns with 20,000 to 50,000 people

○ towns with more than 50,000 people

▬ coalfields

➤ major sea-trade routes

Aberdeen ○

Dundee ○

Glasgow
Paisley ○   ○ Edinburgh

Newcastle-upon-Tyne ○   *Coal to London*

Leeds ○   ○ Hull *Northern Europe*
Liverpool ○ ○ Manchester
           ○ Sheffield
              ○ Nottingham
Birmingham ○   ○ Norwich

Bristol ○   ○ London
○ Bath

North America   ○ Portsmouth

North America

○ Plymouth

Rich and Poor

In 1750 British society was deeply divided. Some people had inherited land and money and were extremely rich. The rest had to work to earn money, and most of them were poor.

The richest class were the **nobles** and **gentry**. Many owned large country estates and grand homes. They were well-educated, and took part in national and local government as Members of **Parliament** and magistrates (local judges). Some made careers as officers in the army or navy. Others became priests in the **Church of England**. A few settled overseas in lands conquered by the British.

Working hard

Some less wealthy people, such as shopkeepers, merchants, doctors and lawyers, lived quite comfortably. Poorer people had to work hard to earn a living, or they starved. Unlike today, there were no doctors or hospitals to care for them when they were sick, and no pensions or other money to help them when they were old or unemployed.

◄ A shopkeeper from Glasgow, around 1790. She is standing behind the counter of her own small shop, checking the change to give to a customer. Behind her, you can see drawers, packets and containers full of goods for sale – probably herbs, spices, tea and sugar. This picture is in the People's Palace in Glasgow.

In 1750, many poor people were employed by the rich as servants or estate workers. After 1800, they worked in factories or other jobs in towns.

A new middle class

By the early 1800s, a new, wealthy 'middle class' was growing in number. It included engineers, who became rich by selling their new inventions, and factory owners and managers, who made money from industry and played an important part in running the new industrial towns. There were also professional farmers, who rented large areas of land from nobles and managed them as businesses, growing food to sell to people in the factory towns.

POPULATION EXPLOSION

Britain's population increased from around 8.5 million in 1750 to almost 21 million by 1851. This was in part because women from ordinary families got married at a younger age than before, and therefore had more babies. It was also because merchants, wealthy farmers and people with skilled jobs earned enough money to eat well, raise large families, stay healthy and live longer.

▼ A travelling knife-grinder, around 1805. He made a living by wheeling his machine for sharpening knives from village to village. He did not earn much, as can be seen from his tattered clothes.

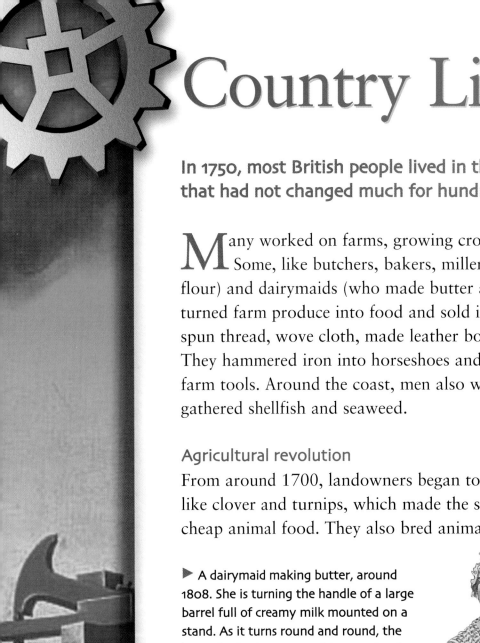

Country Life

In 1750, most British people lived in the countryside in a way that had not changed much for hundreds of years.

Many worked on farms, growing crops and raising animals. Some, like butchers, bakers, millers (who ground grain into flour) and dairymaids (who made butter and cheese from fresh milk), turned farm produce into food and sold it to local customers. Others spun thread, wove cloth, made leather boots or wooden furniture. They hammered iron into horseshoes and cooking pots, or mended farm tools. Around the coast, men also went fishing, while women gathered shellfish and seaweed.

Agricultural revolution

From around 1700, landowners began to experiment with new crops, like clover and turnips, which made the soil more fertile and provided cheap animal food. They also bred animals in a more scientific way to produce bigger, better livestock.

▶ A dairymaid making butter, around 1808. She is turning the handle of a large barrel full of creamy milk mounted on a stand. As it turns round and round, the butterfat in the cream sticks together in lumps. The dairymaid will collect these, add salt, and shape them into neat pats, ready to sell.

Many landowners organised **enclosure schemes**, planting hedges around fields and meadows that before had been open grassland used by all. Traditionally, villagers without a garden or small plot of land of their own had kept cows or pigs on this common land, to feed their families. Now they could no longer do this and many families had less to eat.

Crisis in the countryside

After 1750 farm wages fell: Britain's population was growing rapidly and there were more people looking for jobs. At the same time, new laws designed to help farmers kept the price of grain and bread very high. By 1800, many country people were close to starving. Poor families moved away to the towns in search of work, leaving villages almost deserted.

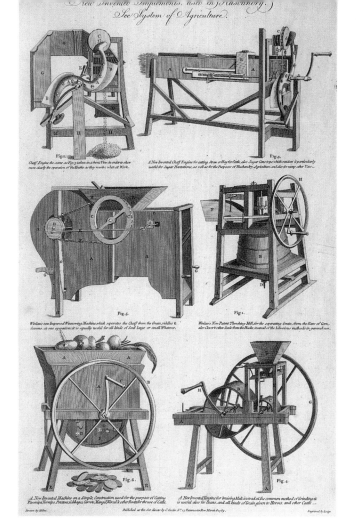

▲ New farm machines, 1789. These machines were all driven by human muscle-power, and were designed to process cereal crops and animal foods.

Even bigger changes came after the canals and railways were built. These opened up new markets for farm produce. Business-like farmers no longer grew a wide range of foods for local people to eat. Instead, they produced foods that they could sell in the towns and make big profits.

◀ This cottage, now in the Museum of Welsh Life at St Fagan's, near Cardiff, was home to a farmworker and his family in Carmarthenshire, Wales, around 1770. Its walls are built of clay and mud, and its roof is thatched with straw. Inside, there are two wooden beds, a dresser, a ladder (to reach the storage space above the beds) and a wheel for spinning woollen thread.

Cities and Towns

During the Industrial Revolution cities and towns grew very quickly, as new industries and foreign trade developed.

Increasing trade between Britain and countries in Asia, Africa and the Americas led to the rapid development of many old port towns, like Bristol and Liverpool, and the growth of new ship-building centres, such as Sunderland. Towns with navy dockyards, such as Portsmouth, also expanded as the government built new warships to fight against foreign enemies. Port growth could be spectacular. Liverpool's population grew from just 6,000 in 1700 to 80,000 by 1800. Many of these new inhabitants were sailors, but there were also ship-builders, rope- and sail-makers, porters, warehousemen, brewers, lodging-house keepers and slave-traders.

▼ Shoppers and strollers throng the busy street of Trongate in Glasgow, 1826. Glasgow was one of the fastest-growing industrial towns, and an important port. Its rich merchants and shopkeepers could afford to build comfortable houses, and buy fine furnishings to go in them. Many of its workers, however, were desperately poor. This picture by John Knox is in the People's Palace, Glasgow.

Fashionable towns

New fashions in leisure and pleasure among wealthy people created many jobs for poorer men and women – as cooks, cleaners, ladies' maids, doctors, gardeners, shopkeepers, dressmakers and entertainers. Rich families liked to spend the summer on their country estates, but preferred to pass the cold, muddy winter months in fashionable county towns such as Chester and York.

From country to town

Poorer country people also flocked to cities and towns, looking for employment. They lived close to the factories, railways, metal **foundries** and coal mines where they worked, in terraces (rows) of small, joined houses, packed tightly together. Whole families often crowded into just one room.

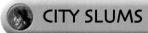

CITY SLUMS

Conditions in industrial cities were grim. Poor people's homes had no drains, indoor lavatories or piped water. They were cold, dark and damp, and infested with rats, **bed-bugs** and **lice**. City air was polluted by fumes from factories, and the streets were muddy and full of rubbish. There were often outbreaks of deadly diseases, such as typhoid (spread by unwashed hands) and cholera (carried in polluted water), which killed many thousands throughout Britain in the 1830s and 1840s. In many industrial towns, half the children died before they were five years old.

▶ Skilled men and women lived in cottages like this iron-worker's house from Merthyr Tydfil, south Wales, now in the Museum of Welsh Life. It is very small, with just a few pieces of simple wooden furniture. It was women's work to care for the family home, even if they also worked at other jobs in factories or mines.

New Ways to Work

Before the Industrial Revolution, most craftspeople worked at home, or in small village workshops. They made all kinds of useful goods, slowly and carefully, by hand.

Often, they sold their goods to merchants, who travelled from village to village, collecting items to sell in the towns. Usually, husbands, wives and children worked together. The work was badly paid, but most families earned enough to survive and control their own lives.

Shift-work and rules

During the Industrial Revolution, machines changed working lives dramatically. Families had to travel to where the machinery was – in factories, foundries, city workshops or mines. In the new industries they had to work for 12 hours or more every day, and could be fined or lose their jobs if they arrived late or left early. They had to follow strict rules, such as not speaking all day.

▼ This scene was painted by an unknown artist between 1775 and 1825 and is now in the Walker Art Gallery in Liverpool. It shows a pit head – the part of a coal-mine that is above the ground. On the left is a steam-powered pump, with a smoking chimney next to the boiler where water was heated to produce the steam. The pump lifted water out of the mine's tunnels, deep underground. In the front of the picture, horses and donkeys pull carts laden with coal.

► Tall, factory buildings at New Lanark in Scotland, 1818. Inside were massive water-powered machines that spun cotton thread. The smaller buildings were homes and schools.

◄ Inside a busy cotton mill (a spinning or weaving factory), 1835. Women and girls are tending dangerous, fast-moving machines that card the raw cotton (comb its rough fibres so they lie straight) and draw it out into strands, ready to spin. All the machines have belts connected to revolving shafts that are turned by steam or water power.

THE LUDDITES

In 1811 and 1812, gangs of skilled hand-weavers in Yorkshire, Lancashire and the Midlands smashed steam-powered spinning and weaving machines, and set factories on fire. They were protesting because the new machines had taken away their work. The protesters were led by a man who called himself 'King Lud' or 'Ned Lud', so they became known as 'Luddites'. Soldiers were called in to stop the riots, and many Luddites were arrested. Seventeen were executed, and many more were **transported** to Australia.

Factory work – good or bad? Workers could no longer use their experience to improve goods as they worked. They lost the responsibility for completing a whole task. Instead each worker might only tighten a few screws, or fit two or three parts of a machine together. Even so, many men and women welcomed factory work. They were desperate to find a job. And, compared with farm work and home craft-work, factory work was well-paid.

Family Life

During the Industrial Revolution, few people lived alone. Most did not want to. Without a family to help them, they would find it very difficult to survive.

The children of the rich were cared for by nursemaids and nannies. They were taught at home by tutors, or sent to boarding schools. Later they often married partners chosen by their parents for political or financial reasons. Poor children helped their parents at work or went out to work themselves. Many never learned to read or write. They were usually free to choose whom they married.

Working families

Women and girls from well-off families did not work for wages but they helped their families by being polite and charming, and entertaining people who were important for their husbands' or fathers' careers.

▼ A dame school (a school owned and run by an unmarried or widowed woman) painted in 1840 by Thomas Webster. Provided their parents could afford the fees, many children learned to read and write at small, local schools like these. Running a dame school was one of the few ways in which a woman could make a career.

Poorer women worked as hard as men, even when they had young children or aged parents to care for. After around 1750, most families stopped working together. Instead, they did different jobs, sometimes for different employers.

▲ A small boy holds open a trapdoor in an underground tunnel so that another boy and girl can push a heavy coal-wagon through it. Pictures like this, from an 1842 report into working conditions in factories and mines, shocked the government into passing laws to protect working children and women.

Working children were asked to do tasks that adults were too big for, such as crawling underneath spinning machines to mend broken threads, climbing up chimneys to clear them of soot, or crouching in dark tunnels to operate trapdoors in mines. Many suffered terrible injuries, and thousands died.

Factory work allowed young, unmarried working women to become more independent than women from richer families. They earned their own wages and, although they gave most of the money to their parents, they still had some left to spend as they chose.

▲ A housemaid in about 1808. Many young, unmarried women worked as servants in big houses belonging to the wealthy. At the age of about 14, they left their families to live with their employers. Their wages were very low but they received free food and lodgings.

THE FACTORY ACTS

After 1819, the British government began to pass laws, called the Factory Acts, to protect women and children at work. By 1844 children aged 9-13 were restricted to 6.5 hours' work a day, and older children and women to 12 hours' a day. Women and children under 10 were banned from working in mines, and young children were no longer allowed to work in mills and cloth factories. All moving machines in factories had to have safety barriers.

Food and Drink

The Industrial Revolution led to many changes in the way British food was produced. By 1850, for the first time, people were buying most of their food from shops.

In 1750, families living in the countryside produced much of their own food. They grew fruit and vegetables in gardens, and gathered wild nuts and berries. Most families kept chickens to provide eggs, and perhaps also a pig for meat, or a cow to give milk. If they worked on a farm, they might be given one meal every day, or some of their wages might be paid in food. Their biggest food expenses were flour from the local mill, which they used to bake rough, brown bread, and beer from the local brewery.

▼ The kitchen of a rich farming family's house at Pockerley Manor (today part of the Beamish North of England Open Air Museum), around 1825. Meals were cooked on the cast-iron range (left) and kettles were boiled over an open fire. Pots, pans, plates and dishes were neatly stored on shelves around the walls. There were no refrigerators or freezers – and no kitchen sink. Dishes were washed in a separate room, called a scullery, close by.

Food from shops

The Industrial Revolution changed this. In cities, people had no way of producing their own foods. Instead they used the wages they earned in factories to buy food. There were no tinned foods, refrigerators or fast lorries, and the food was often stale or rotten after a long journey from the countryside. It was also often mixed with dangerous chemicals, such as **lead** and **alum**, to keep it looking fresh, or to make it last longer. Shop food was very expensive and many unskilled workers earned only enough to buy bread or potatoes.

Food for poor and rich

Most people's meals were very plain – for example, bread and cheese, or vegetable soup. The poorest, with no gardens, no work and no money, often went hungry.

Rich people's meals were very different. Wealthy families employed expert cooks to produce large meals for themselves and their guests. They could afford meat, butter, cream, cakes and pastries, and they paid gardeners to grow fruits and fresh vegetables all year round. They also enjoyed wine, brandy and imported luxuries, such as tea, coffee, chocolate and sugar.

▼ A town baker, about 1808. He is carrying two wicker (woven twig) baskets full of freshly-baked bread, which he will sell from door to door. Poor people ate far more bread than we do today.

Fashion and Working Clothes

Throughout the Industrial Revolution, you could tell how rich someone was by looking at their clothes.

Fashions for wealthy women changed quite rapidly, from stiff silk gowns with low-cut **bodices** and tight waists, to loose lightweight dresses, made from a delicate Indian cotton called muslin. After 1830, heavy, fitted dresses became popular again, this time with wide, padded sleeves.

Men's clothes changed too, from long jackets and ankle-length greatcoats, worn with knee-length trousers, to tight **tail-coats** and skin-tight full-length trousers called pantaloons.

From around 1750, men and women wore wigs, often powdered to look fashionably grey. The fashion then changed to loose curls for both sexes and then to **ringlets** for women, and short hair with bushy side-whiskers for men. Fashionable men and women also wore hats, gloves, **corsets**, perfume, make-up and jewellery.

▲ In this painting by Rolinda Sharples, fashionable men and women gather for a ball at the Assembly Rooms in Clifton, near Bristol, in 1818. The women wear high-waisted gowns of silk or muslin, with flat slippers on their feet. The men wear coats with tails or army officers' uniforms.

Plain and simple

Poorer people's clothes were more plain. They were also much easier to move around in and work in. Women wore dresses with close-fitting bodices, tight waists and full skirts, and kept warm with thick woollen shawls. Men wore baggy, full-length trousers, collarless shirts, short waist-coats and jackets. On their feet, working men and women wore strong boots, pattens (metal platforms, that raised the feet above puddles and mud) or wooden-soled **clogs**.

Most clothes were hand-sewn by women at home, or made in **sweatshops**, where skilled women and girls worked long hours, in damp, dusty conditions, with poor light and no fresh air.

Until around 1830, ordinary clothes were mostly made of linen or wool. But after 1830, cotton cloth, mass-produced in factories, was cheaper and more popular. It was also much easier to wash and dry.

DANGEROUS CLOTHES

Factory-workers had to be careful what they wore. Loose hair, or trailing skirts or sleeves, could easily get trapped and drag the wearer into fast-moving machinery. Sweatshops (crowded workshops) had no ventilation and workers passed infections between themselves. Many sweatshop workers died from chest infections. Girls who started lace-making and fine white embroidery at the age of 8 often lost their sight before they were 30. Making some clothes involved dangerous chemicals. Top hats required poisonous mercury (a silvery, liquid metal), which permanently damaged hat-makers' brains. That is where the expression 'mad as a hatter' comes from.

▼ The latest men's fashions, 1815. The man second from left is wearing wellington boots. These were named after a famous army commander, the Duke of Wellington (1769-1852), who had defeated the French at the Battle of Waterloo earlier that year. All the men have top hats, and those on the far left and the far right are wearing tail-coats.

Entertainments

As towns grew during the Industrial Revolution, they provided many new opportunities for people to enjoy themselves.

◀ In this picture by James Pollard, crowds gather in front of the grandstand at Epsom race-course, in Surrey, 1830. Both rich and poor people liked to spend 'a day at the races', watching the horses run and betting on which would win.

During the winter, it was usual for the rich to spend several weeks in fashionable towns. There they amused themselves by shopping, visiting art galleries and museums, going to concerts and theatres, and dancing at parties or balls. They also won and lost vast sums of money playing cards. Dramatic and romantic novels were very popular among those women who could read.

In some towns, like Bath, visitors combined pleasure with the search for good health. They visited spas (comfortable health centres) to drink water from natural springs. This often smelled and tasted horrible, but people believed it had medicinal powers. In London, pleasure gardens (landscaped parks where many entertainments were provided) were open to any suitably dressed person who could pay the entrance fee.

Smaller cities, like York and Norwich, built elegant assembly rooms, for public meetings, lectures, dances and concerts. On special occasions, important people or city councils paid for public firework displays.

For less wealthy townspeople there were street musicians and **ballad**-singers, stalls selling cheap take-away foods and, for men only, inns and drinking houses. Crowds gathered to watch wrestling and boxing matches, and also gruesome spectacles like public hangings. People also enjoyed sports like **cock-fighting** that we would think very cruel today.

Country fun

In the country, working people strolled around the stalls and sideshows at traditional fairs and celebrated harvest home (the end of the farming year) with feasting, music and songs. Travelling musicians also played for country dances, and travelling theatre groups staged plays in barns and on village greens.

BESIDE THE SEASIDE

After around 1800, sea bathing became fashionable for wealthy families, who believed the sea air and salty water were good for their health. In new resorts like Brighton, Sidmouth and Lyme Regis they were carried into the water in covered wagons. Then, fully dressed in bathing clothes – dresses or shirts and trousers but made of strong, washable fabric – they were dipped into the water.

▼ A couple enjoying a country fair, around 1800. They are listening to an old man who is playing a tune on bells held in his hands, and fastened to his clothes. In the background, people are watching a stage show.

Soldiers, Sailors and the Police

For much of the period between 1750 and 1850, Britain was at war. In the 18th century British troops fought for the right to rule in India and Canada, and lost a war against rebels in America. Later, from 1793 to 1815, Britain fought a long campaign against France.

All these foreign wars meant that the British army and navy needed a steady supply of recruits (new soldiers and sailors). Officers came from the poorest, least powerful gentry families. They hoped to win fame and make their fortunes in a dangerous, but honourable, career. The men these officers commanded were recruited from the poorest groups in society. Sometimes they volunteered for service. Often they were tricked into joining by accepting a drink or other gift containing the king's shilling (a hidden coin that represented army wages). Or they might be kidnapped by a press gang. This was a bunch of tough recruiting officers, who snatched away young men, and forced them to join the navy.

◀ A recruiting sergeant, dressed in a splendid uniform, tries to persuade young village men to join the army in 1813, at the height of Britain's war with France. One young man is trying on a soldier's cap.

▲ A picture by J H Atkinson of sailors at morning prayers. On the right of the picture, you can see Admiral Lord Nelson (with bandaged head and star-shaped badge on his chest). Nelson defeated the French in many battles. He was killed during the Battle of Trafalgar in 1805.

Life in the army and navy

Most recruits were shocked by the hardships and dangers of their new life. Soldiers spent most of their lives abroad, living in crowded barracks or unhealthy camps. Food was poor, discipline was fierce, pay was low and medical treatment was savage. Life in the navy was also harsh. Sailors had to endure cold, wet, rotten food and sickness on board ship, and face storms, shipwrecks and terrifying **broadsides** from enemy cannons.

Dangerous times

At home, crime was rising in the crowded cities. In 1829 the government created the first police force. Working men were recruited as police constables. The new 'peelers' or 'bobbies', as they were called, soon became familiar figures as they patrolled the streets, dressed in top hats and dark-blue tail-coats and carrying a wooden stick called a truncheon.

▼ In this cartoon a new policeman arrests suspects outside a police station in 1830. In London, police stations were set up in many areas.

Religion, Death and Burial

In 1750, Britain was officially a Christian country. But Christian worship did not mean the same thing to everyone, and some people had no religious faith.

In England, the Church of England was the official form of Christianity. Many priests were the sons of wealthy families, who hoped the Church would provide them with a peaceful, pleasant, scholarly career. They did not give people much spiritual guidance – or even practical help when they were hungry, homeless or unemployed.

▲ A young Quaker girl carrying a Bible, painted in about 1830 by Isaac Pollock. Quakers and Methodists stressed the importance of Bible study, and used Bible teachings to guide their everyday lives. This painting can be seen in the Victoria & Albert Museum in London.

Quakers and Methodists

There were also unofficial Christian groups. The two most influential were the Society of Friends (nicknamed 'Quakers') and the Methodists. Quakers held prayer meetings, where men and women sat quietly until their consciences urged them to speak. There were no priests or leaders. Everyone was treated with equal respect. Methodists organised large, open-air assemblies. Travelling preachers gave rousing **sermons**, and everyone sang loud, enthusiastic hymns. By 1850, Methodists had built many chapels for Sunday worship, especially in Wales.

Christian care

Methodist and Quaker ideas inspired many social reformers, such as anti-slavery campaigner William Wilberforce and prison reformer Elizabeth Fry. Another was newspaper owner Robert Raikes, who set up Sunday Schools in towns where child factory-workers could learn about religion – and how to read and write – on their day off.

▲ In 1807 Parliament banned the slave trade in countries ruled by Britain, and in 1833 freed all slaves in Britain. After these successes, anti-slavery protesters tried to end slavery worldwide. They came together in this meeting at Exeter Hall in London in 1841.

Death and funerals

Traditionally, the dead were buried after a funeral service held in a church or a chapel. But after around 1800, wealthy families also paid funeral directors to organise elaborate funerals, with horse-drawn processions and floral tributes. They asked for the dead to be buried in new, landscaped cemeteries, rather than within church grounds. An impressive, well-organised funeral became a mark of respectability. Everyone – even poor families – carefully observed mourning customs, such as hanging black curtains at windows and wearing dark-coloured clothes.

◀ Inside the Unitarian chapel from Drefach Felindre, Carmarthenshire (now in the Museum of Welsh Life at St Fagan's). Unitarians were an unofficial Christian group. The worshippers sat behind the wooden partitions, and musicians played in the upstairs gallery.

New Ideas

The Industrial Revolution was a time of great experiments and discoveries. New inventions and forms of transport opened up exciting possibilities for both rich and poor.

It was a big step for a poor country family to leave their home and seek work in a nearby town. A few adventurous families left Britain altogether, to settle in North America, Asia and the Caribbean. Some were driven by hunger or homelessness, but others hoped to make their fortunes.

Changing society

Advances in science made people think that the lives of the poor might also be changed for the better. Factory owner Robert Owen, who ran the New Lanark mills in Scotland (see page 13), tried to create a 'model community' there, with shorter working hours, good housing and free education for children and adults. He established a village store where workers could buy goods cheaply. The profits from the store helped to pay for the schools.

▼ A dancing class at the Institute for the Formation of Character (a leisure and study centre) in New Lanark, painted by G Hunt in around 1828. A small number of factory owners like Robert Owen cared for their workers, and encouraged them to spend time improving their lives by learning new skills.

Political changes taking place in Europe led to calls for changes in the way British government worked and for the reform of Parliament. Only country landowners, and some property owners who lived in towns that had existed before the Industrial Revolution, had the right to vote or become Members of Parliament. People in the new industrial cities, whether rich or poor, had no vote at all. Campaigners thought that more people should be able to vote.

▲ In 1819, soldiers charged into a crowd of 60,000 peaceful protesters supporting Parliamentary reform in St Peter's Fields, Manchester. Eleven people were killed and over 400 were injured. George Cruikshank drew this cartoon of the incident, which became known as the 'Peterloo Massacre'.

▲ A trade union emblem of the Glasgow Association of Cotton Spinners, painted on a tin tray around 1820. It is now in the People's Palace, Glasgow. Its motto reveals the members' hopes: 'Success to the cotton tree! Success to the Friendly Association of Cotton Spinners! Success to commerce!'

In 1832, a new law reformed Parliament and gave a small number of middle-class, property-owning men, including those in industrial areas, the right to vote. But most men, and all women, still could not vote.

At this time working men and women also joined together in the first **trade unions** to campaign for better pay, shorter hours and safer working conditions.

Legacy

Many of the inventions and ideas of the Industrial Revolution still affect our lives today.

New canals, railways and steamships linked distant parts of Britain more closely together, and helped develop British industry by carrying raw materials to factories and finished goods to markets. They put British people in touch with lands overseas, encouraging many of them to seek work abroad, and helping the British government to build a worldwide empire.

▲ This fine china jug was made in a pottery factory in Coalport, Shropshire, in 1828. It is decorated with a picture of the world's first cast-iron bridge, built by Abraham Darby in 1779 at Coalbrookdale, Shropshire.

◄ During the Industrial Revolution, barges and narrow-boats carried heavy, bulky cargoes such as coal and pottery along Britain's canals. Today, many of these old boats have been carefully restored, and are used as houseboats, or hired for holiday trips. These canal boats are at Little Venice in London.

People today still belong to trade unions, or to other organisations that aim to protect workers' rights. These were first set up during the Industrial Revolution when ordinary people realised that, by joining together to take action, they would have more power. The Co-operative movement, founded in 1844 to help workers, still runs shops and inspires many community projects.

Changing lifestyles

The Industrial Revolution changed the way most people lived. Today we generally live in towns. Most people leave their homes to go out to work and earn money wages, instead of being paid with goods. Almost all people buy their food, rather than growing it at home. We also use mass-production techniques, invented during the Industrial Revolution, to make millions of identical items, from CDs to plastic toothbrushes, cheaply and quickly. Factory-style production techniques are even used to organise supermarkets and farms. All these trends began during the Industrial Revolution.

INDUSTRIAL REVOLUTION SURVIVALS

We can still see early steam-powered machines and re-created workers' homes in museums and heritage centres. Carefully-preserved factories and mills are open to the public. We can travel along roads, canals and railways built by Industrial Revolution pioneers. And modern life would be very different without one of the Industrial Revolution's most important inventions – rolled steel, which is used today to make everything from cars and washing machines to baked bean cans.

▼ Today we can visit many old buildings that have survived from the time of the Industrial Revolution, like the house of mill-owner Robert Owen at New Lanark in Scotland. Robert Owen's work at New Lanark encouraged the Co-operative movement.

Timeline

1712 Thomas Newcomen invents the first steam engine.

1733 John Kay invents the flying shuttle, an automatic device to speed up weaving.

1761 First major canal opens near Manchester.

1764 James Hargreaves invents the spinning jenny, a machine to spin thread.

1765, 1782 James Watt invents more efficient steam engines.

1769 Richard Arkwright invents a water-powered weaving machine.

1779 Samuel Crompton invents the mule, a thread-spinning machine.

1779 Abraham Darby III builds the first cast-iron bridge at Coalbrookdale.

1780s First tarred roads laid by James MacAdam in Scotland.

1799 Marc Brunel opens the first mass-production factory.

1799 The first trade unions are banned.

1807 Slave trade banned in British colonies.

1811-1812 Luddites smash new machines.

1819 Protesters calling for the right to vote are killed at 'Peterloo Massacre', in Manchester.

1829 First passenger railway opens (Stockton to Darlington) with locomotives designed by George Stephenson. Robert Peel creates a police force to combat crime.

1832 First Parliamentary Reform Act allows more (mostly wealthy) men to vote.

1833 First Factory Act restricts the working hours of women and children.

1837 Samuel Morse sends the first British telegraph message.

1837 First steamship *Great Western*, designed by Isambard Kingdom Brunel, sails across the Atlantic Ocean.

1838 Chartist movement demands votes for all men.

1839 First national postal service set up.

1842 Mines Act bans women and children from working underground.

Places to Visit

Beamish North of England Open Air Museum, Beamish, County Durham
Many 19th-century houses, shops, factories and schools.

Black Country Living Museum, Dudley, West Midlands
Re-creates the experiences of people who worked in industrial towns.

Brighton, East Sussex
The top seaside resort in Industrial Revolution times, with many fine houses and an amazing pavilion.

Cornwall Industrial Discovery Centre, Pool
Information about mining and important early inventions.

Ironbridge Gorge Museums Trust, Coalbrookdale, Shropshire
The site of Abraham Darby's steel-making discovery, and the world's first cast-iron bridge.

National Railway Museum, York
Shows how railways developed and displays many historic locomotives.

National Waterways Museum, Gloucester
Tells the story of Britain's canals.

New Lanark Experience, New Lanark, South Lanarkshire
Robert Owen's pioneering new community for industrial workers.

Ragged School Museum, London
What school was like for children who worked in factories.

SS Great Britain, Bristol
Brunel's famous iron ship, powered by a steam-driven propeller.

Scottish Mining Museum, Newtongrange, Midlothian
Tells how men, women and children dug for coal deep underground.

Sir Richard Arkwright's Cromford Mill, Cromford, Derbyshire
One of the most important factories to survive from the Industrial Revolution.

Summerlee Heritage Park, Coatbridge, North Lanarkshire
Working displays of many industrial inventions.

Glossary

alum a chemical containing potassium and aluminium.

ballad a popular song that tells a story.

bed-bugs insects that live in bedding, biting people and sucking their blood.

bodice the part of a woman's dress above the waist.

broadside a number of guns or cannons all fired at the same time.

cast iron the substance produced when iron ore is heated with coke or coal until it melts, then poured into moulds to set.

Church of England a branch of the Christian Church headed by the ruling king or queen of England. It is the 'official' religion of England.

clogs strong boots or shoes with wooden soles.

cock-fighting a cruel sport in which two male chickens were made to fight one another by stabbing and scratching with their long sharp claws. The losing chicken usually died.

corset a close-fitting bodice, often strengthened with whalebone.

enclosure schemes landowners' plans to surround large areas of open grassland with fences.

foundries factories where iron is smelted (made) from iron ore (rock containing iron) and coke.

gentry people from rich, landowning families. Not so grand or powerful as nobles.

lead a grey metal that melts and bends easily. It is very poisonous.

lice insects that infest human hair and skin and spread diseases.

mass-produce to make lots of identical objects very quickly by machine.

nobles people from rich landowning families, often with titles such as 'lord' and 'lady'.

Parliament a national assembly which discusses and decides government policy and makes new laws.

raw materials substances such as iron or wool that are processed in factories to create finished goods.

ringlets long, twisted curls.

sermons religious talks.

sweatshops crowded, unhealthy workshops.

tail-coat a tight-fitting coat, worn by men. It was short at the front but had two thigh-length panels, known as 'tails', at the back.

trade union group of workers who join together to campaign for better pay and working conditions.

transported forcibly taken to live in another country.

Books and Websites

Books

Sean Connelly, *The Industrial Revolution*, Heinemann Library, 2003

Terry Deary, *The Gorgeous Georgians*, Scholastic, 1998

Peter Hepplewhite and M Campbell, *All About The Industrial Revolution*, Hodder Wayland, 2002

N Keyy, R Rees and J Shuter, *The Industrial Revolution*, Heinemann Library, 1998

Fiona Macdonald, *Women in 19th Century Europe*, Belitha, 1999

Websites

www.ironbridge.org.uk
The official site of the Ironbridge Trust, with lots of information about the early years of the Industrial Revolution.

www.bbc.co.uk/schools/victorians
Lives of 19th-century people, at work, at home and at school.

www.womeninworldhistory.com/lesson7
Women's and girls' lives during the Industrial Revolution.

www.fordham.edu/halsall/modsbook14
Visual and written evidence from the Industrial Revolution era.

www.bbc.co.uk/history/society_culture /industrialisation
A site for adults, but with a great deal of fascinating information and many interactive features.

Index